HARMONICA

by Ralph Agresta

The original just got better!
Full-band backup to 12 extended jams in authentic
rock, blues, and country styles. Includes an overview of
harmonica techniques, plus tips on scales and riffs to use
with each track. In standard notation and
easy-to-use harmonica tablature.

Cover photography by Randall Wallace

This book Copyright © 1997 by Amsco Publications,
A Division of Music Sales Corporation, New York

Order No. AM 945318
US International Standard Book Number: 0.8256.1641.7
UK International Standard Book Number: 0.7119.6752.0

Exclusive Distributors:
Music Sales Corporation
257 Park Avenue South, New York, NY 10010 USA
Music Sales Limited
8/9 Frith Street, London W1V 5TZ England
Music Sales Pty. Limited
120 Rothschild Street, Rosebery, Sydney, NSW 2018, Australia

Printed in the United States of America by
Vicks Lithograph and Printing Corporation

Amsco Publications
New York/London/Sydney

£7 95

CD Track Listing

1. I'll See Ya Later
2. You Really Gotta Love Me
3. Waiting On My Lady
4. Plantation Blues
5. Rockabilly Truth
6. Daydreamin'
7. Honky Tonk Groove
8. Twelve-Bar Blues in E
9. Twelve-Bar Blues in A
10. Twenty-Four-Bar Blues in G
11. Twelve-Bar Very Slow Swing in G
12. The Hindenburg Medley

Contents

Introduction

The harmonica is one of the world's most adaptable instruments. Not only is it convenient to carry and play, but its soulful and expressive sound has earned it a place in almost every type of music, from blues to jazz to country to classical.

Hi! I'm Ralph Agresta. With the growing popularity of my *JamTrax* series, we've received tons of positive feedback and numerous requests to make packages for other instruments. (Our first eight were generally guitar oriented.) For this *JamTrax for Harmonica* I've selected a dozen of the best *JamTrax* tracks for harmonica playing in a variety styles.

Everyone knows that the best way to improve musical skills is to play with a live band, and now you can do just that in the privacy of your own room. Join me (on guitar), and my friends John Abbey (on bass), Phil Ricciardi (on keyboards), Larry Wurtzel (on trumpet), Michael Alexander (on sax), and either Ernie Finamore or Chris Carroll (on drums) for twelve harmonica-friendly jams. We'll be the backup band and you add the harmonica parts and solos. Experienced players will enjoy using this disc to experiment with new ideas and techniques or for warming up before gigs. Beginners can practice without the pressure that often comes from playing in front of other people.

Inside this book you'll find, along with suggested riff and solo samples, simple charts with chord symbols that will guide you through the structure of each jam.

Good luck, have fun, and, as always, I sincerely hope that you enjoy and learn from this book and CD.

Playing the Harmonica

Most harmonica instruction books have songs that are all arranged in one key (usually C), so that the beginning harp student can get started with only one harp. We, however, opted to include tracks in four of the more popular harmonica keys. We think that this approach enables us to represent the kinds of keys and styles that a harmonica player should be prepared to encounter. So, to enjoy this package fully you will need four harmonicas, one each in the keys of C, D, A, and F.

Let's begin with a brief look at the basics of harmonica playing and notation. This book was written for the common diatonic (ten-hole) harmonica, and we'll be using one in the key of C for this review. (If you are a true novice and feel that you need some more detailed basic instruction, we recommend the book *You Can Play Harmonica* (published by Amsco). The hole numbers are indicated below the actual notation, so this should really help if you're not a great reader. Notice in the first example that a circled hole number indicates a "draw" note (a note sounded by sucking), and an uncircled number indicates a "blow" note (a note sounded by blowing). Blow and draw these simple chords as an example.

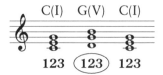

This C major scale represents a sample of single-note harmonica notation.

In the charts and suggestions that follow we've limited the use of bends to the easier "drawbends" that in most cases are simple half- and whole-step bends. The slurs (lines) over the groups of notes indicate that you should play them in one breath.

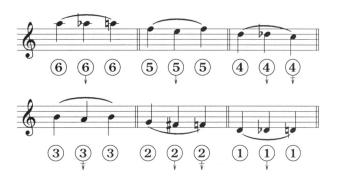

Beginners should not get too hung up on bending notes. Note bending can be very tricky and will take time to master. If you have trouble bending notes as you try the suggested patterns, simply play the principal notes. For those of you who want to investigate every note-bending possibility, here's a comprehensive chart. Knock yourself out!

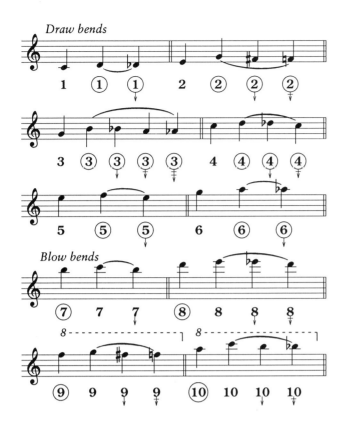

It's important to remember that the relative order of pitches is the same from one harmonica to another (i.e., if you can play one key of harmonica, you can play all the others as well). Be sure to try to play every lick you learn in as many keys as you have harmonicas. Here's a list of the principal notes on the four harmonicas we'll be using.

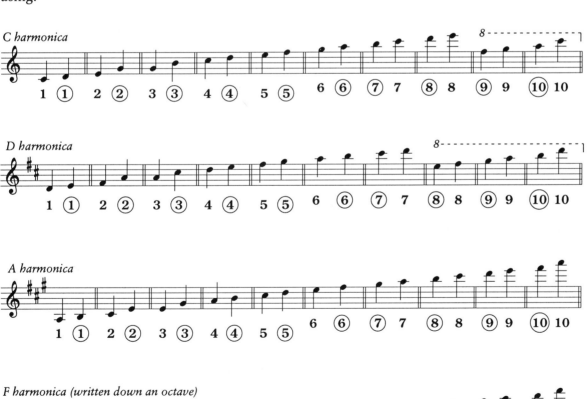

I'll See Ya Later

C harmonica, second position

We'll start with a fast swing blues, the first of four Chicago-style tracks. For the introduction you can play what's written on the chart or have a listen and prepare some of your own ideas.

Pattern 1: A section variation

Notice how well this works with the saxophone part that you hear on every other A section. Don't be afraid to try your own variations on this idea.

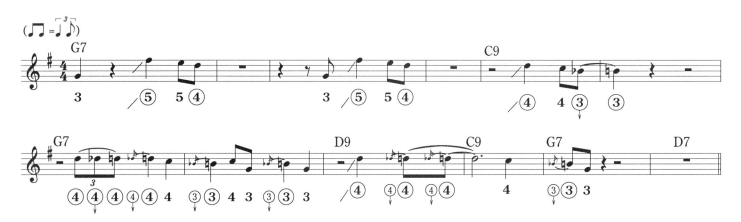

Patterns 2 and 3: Trills

You execute a trill by rapidly and evenly alternating between two tones. The first bar of each example shows the trill as we will notate it in this book; the second bar is to give you an idea of what you will be playing.

pattern 2

pattern 3

Pattern 4: Coda variation

Here's another part that you can play over the coda.

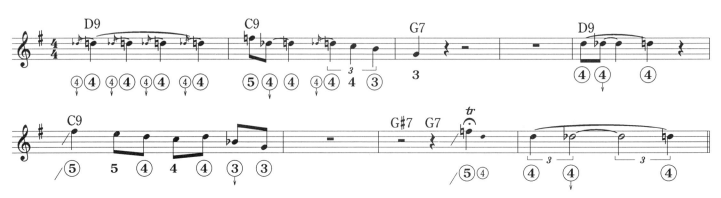

I'll See Ya Later

You Really Got to Love Me

D harmonica, second position

This second Chicago-style blues track is in 12/8 time, which you can think of as 4/4 with a srong triplet feel. Keep in mind that the Chicago-style players play their "harps" through microphones directly plugged in to small amps. When these amps are cranked up loud they produce a raunchy, distorted sound.

Patterns 1 and 2: Motive (main lick)

Pattern 1 features the main lick without bends. Pattern 2, adding bends, is a bluesier approach to the same lick.

pattern 1

pattern 2

Pattern 3: Riff sample

This four-bar sample will fit just about anywhere in the track, but works especially well in measures 21 through 24.

Pattern 4: Another trill

Here again we see a trill written two ways. Try this one over measures 15-17 or 19--21.

You Really Got to Love Me

Waiting on My Lady

F harmonica, second position
Harmonica part written down an octave

This track is a basic twelve-bar blues with a straight $\frac{4}{4}$ time feel. The three patterns that follow are meant to be played consecutively over cycles 1, 2, and 3, and 5, 6, and 7. Save cycles 4 and 8 for some freestyle soloing.

Pattern 1: Rhythmic double stops
This example shows how double stops (two notes played at once) can be used rhythmically to accent the chord changes.

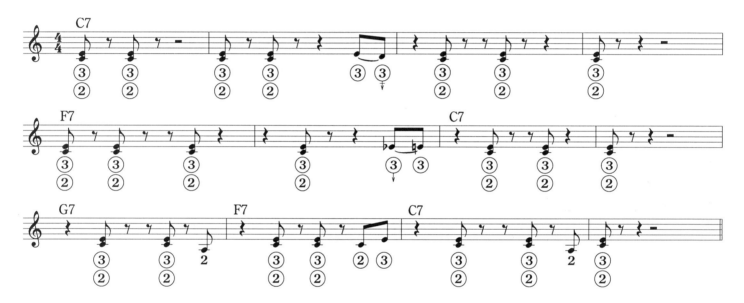

Pattern 2: Motive (main lick)
Here's another twelve-bar example featuring a main lick which is varied slightly to cover an entire cycle.

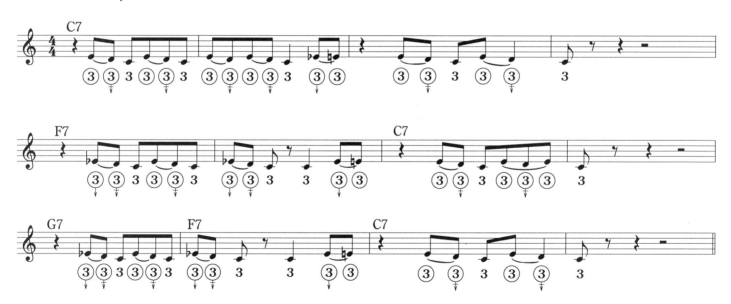

Pattern 3: Three riff samples

These three riffs are placed to create a "question-and-answer" approach to coloring
the progression. If you're jamming with a friend who's playing another instrument
or even a second harmonica, have him or her fill the first two measures of each line.
You can play these licks as an answer to their musical questions.

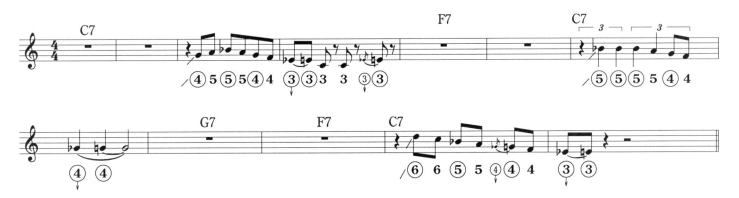

Pattern 4: Riff sample

Try this over the last two measures of the last cycle to end the track.

Waiting on My Lady

Brisk straight-eighth feel

Plantation Blues

F harmonica, second position
Harmonica part written down an octave

This fourth and final Chicago blues-style track features two sections. The $\boxed{\text{A}}$ section can be dealt with by playing variations of the main riff. The $\boxed{\text{B}}$ section is where you'll want to break out into a full-fledged solo.

Patterns 1, 2, and 3: Half- and whole-step bend riffs

These three lines each feature a variation on the main riff played with both half- and whole-step bends.

pattern 1

pattern 2

pattern 3

Pattern 4: $\boxed{\text{B}}$ section solo suggestion

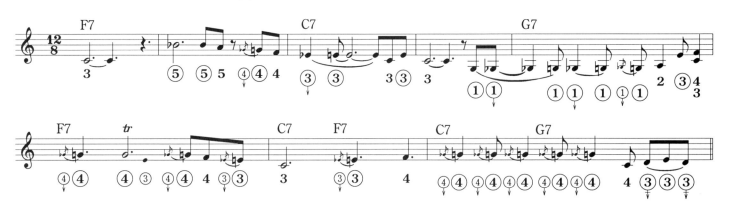

Pattern 5: Riff sample

This two-bar riff may be used over the third ending to finish the song.

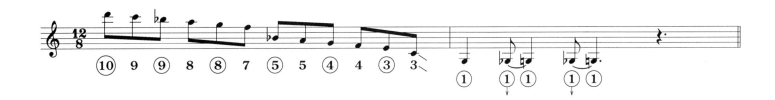

Plantation Blues

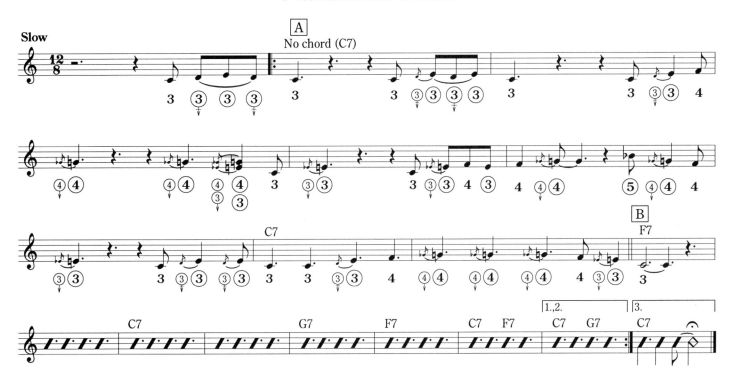

Rockabilly Truth

A harmonica, second position

Pattern 1: Rhythmic double stops

Double stops like these can be used anywhere throughout this rockabilly-style track, but when played in the intro they set up the first verse very nicely.

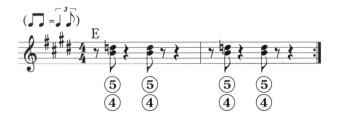

Pattern 2: Solo suggestion

Pattern 3: Alternate solo suggestion

This example contains double stops and triads. No doubt you already know that it's usually more difficult to play single notes on a harmonica than whole chords. If you find that some of your single notes accidentally become double stops, use these happy accidents as long as they sound good. Listen to some of Bob Dylan's or Neil Young's harmonica work to hear this kind of chordal playing.

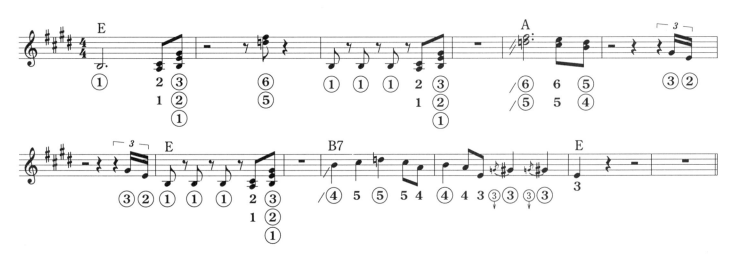

Pattern 4: Riff sample

This flashy riff is technically difficult and will require some serious practice to get up
to speed. Pay close attention attention to your alternate breathing and have fun!

simile

Pattern 5: Riff sample

Try this over the last three bars of the tune (7th ending).

Rockabilly Truth

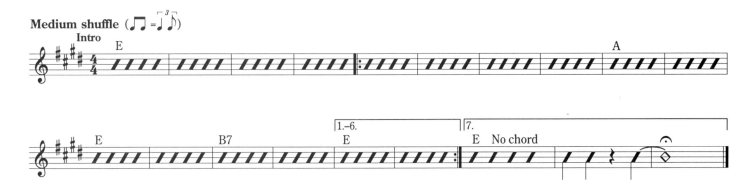

Daydreamin'

F harmonica, first position
Harmonica part written down an octave

Up until now we've been playing in second position. Such an approach, popularly known as "cross-harping," involves (as you may have already noticed) using a harmonica that is up a fourth from the key the song is in. For example, if the song is in the key of G you use a C harp. If the song is in the key of E you use an A harp, and so on.

On this track we're going to play in first position. This means that the song and the harmonica are in the same key. Many harmonica instruction booklets are written mostly this way, and this is usually the approach beginners take when they get their first harmonica. While second position is right for that bluesy sound, first position lends itself more to a diatonic setting. This track, a country tune, is just that kind of setting. For it we've offered two charts with two slightly different melodic treatments. Try mixing and matching licks from each.

Daydreamin' (version 1)

Daydreamin' (version 2)

Honky Tonk Groove

C harmonica, second position

This is our first rock and roll-style track. We'll be cross-harping again in the key of G, so get out your C harp. Although rock harmonica playing is very similar to blues playing, one notable difference is that rock players often use their harps to mimic horn lines. You'll find samples of "hornlike" harmonica parts in the next three patterns.

Pattern 1: Eight-bar hornlike riff

This sample will fit right over the full eight-bar chord progression. Remember that notes grouped together under slurs should be played in a single breath.

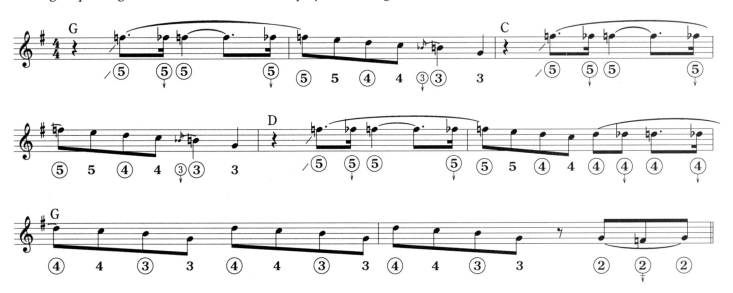

Pattern 2: Two-bar hornlike riff

This riff can be played four times to fill the eight-bar progression.

Pattern 3: Four-bar hornlike pattern

This pair of phrases should be played over the V-I (D-G) change in the second four
bars of the progression.

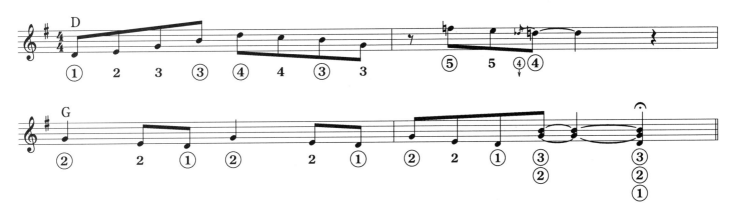

Pattern 4: Flashy riff

Try this one over the V chord (D).

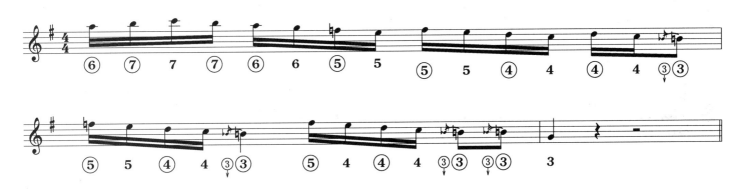

Honky Tonk Groove

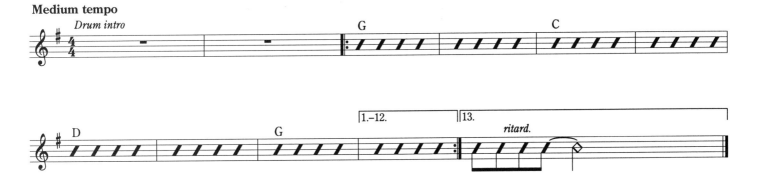

Twelve-Bar Blues in E

A harmonica, second position

We'll be going back to the basic blues on this track.

Patterns 1 and 2: Two Blues Riffs

The riffs contained in these four bars will work well over the four bars of E7 that start the progression, but you can also just repeat them over the entire twelve bars.

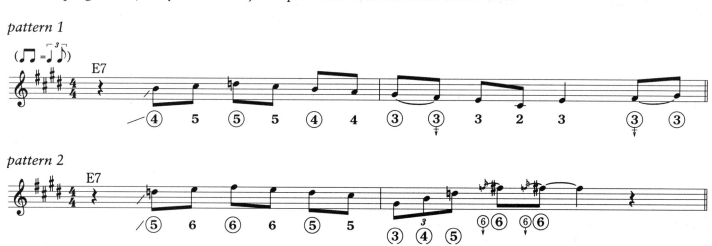

Pattern 3: Double stops

Here's a twelve-bar double-stop part that can be used as a main riff. Play it over an imaginary A section during the odd-numbered choruses, and solo over an imaginary B section during the even-numbered choruses.

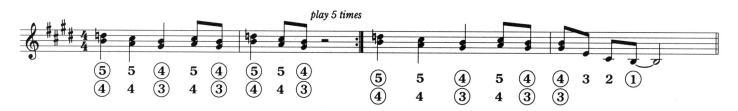

Pattern 4: Triplet riff

The triplets in this riff will require the kind of alternate breathing that we tried earlier ("Rockabilly Truth," pattern 4). Play this pattern over any of the four-bar lines in the chart. The alternate ending notes (in parentheses) should be played when applying this pattern to the V-IV-I-V (B7-A7-E7-B7) changes.

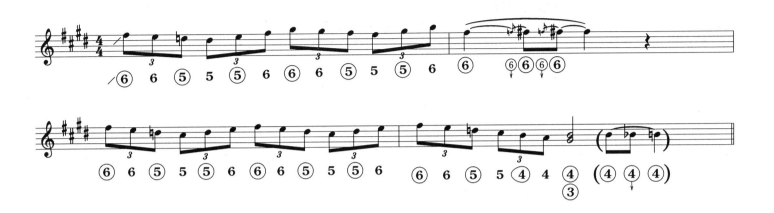

Pattern 5: Coda riff

Try this over the last two measures of the piece.

Twelve-Bar Blues in E

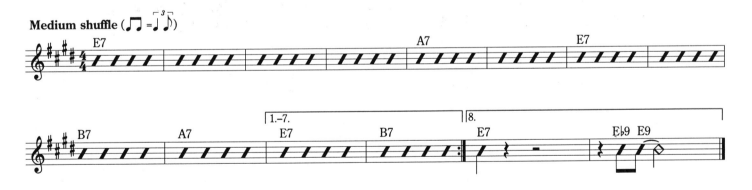

Twelve-Bar Blues in A

D harmonica, second position

This tune has a similar feel to the previous track. Again, we're dealing with a basic twelve-bar blues progression.

Pattern 1: Twelve-bar solo sample

Need we say more? Just play it!

Patterns 2 and 3: Triplet riffs

Like the triplet riff that we saw in "Twelve-Bar Blues in E" (pattern 4), save these flashy lines for a peak moment in your jam.

pattern 2

pattern 3

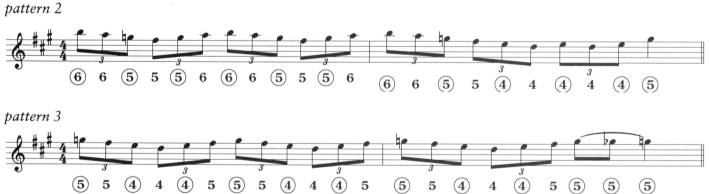

Pattern 4: Coda riff

Use these custom-tailored lines over the last four bars of the tune.

Twelve-Bar Blues in A

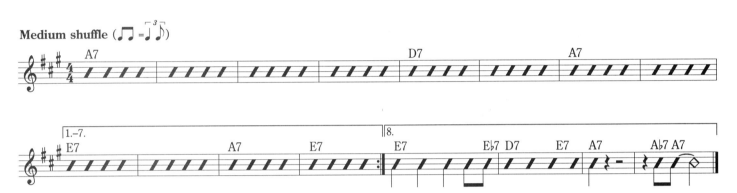

Twenty-Four-Bar Blues in G

C harmonica, second position

Don't be scared by the words "twenty-four." This is still a simple blues progression, with a decidedly rock-and-roll feel. It may remind you of the Stones' "Off the Hook," or of their cover of Bobby Womack's "It's All Over Now."

Pattern 1: Intro riff
Try this over the intro.

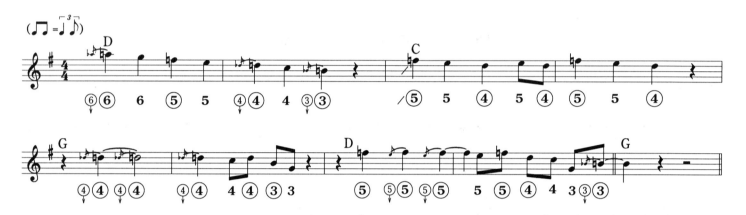

Pattern 2: Verse riffs
Repeat and vary this four-bar ditty throughout the twenty-four-bar verse section.

Pattern 3: Trill riff
Try this one during the choruses where the rhythm guitars open up.

Pattern 4: Coda riff
Save this one for the last bar of the piece.

Twenty-Four-Bar Blues in G

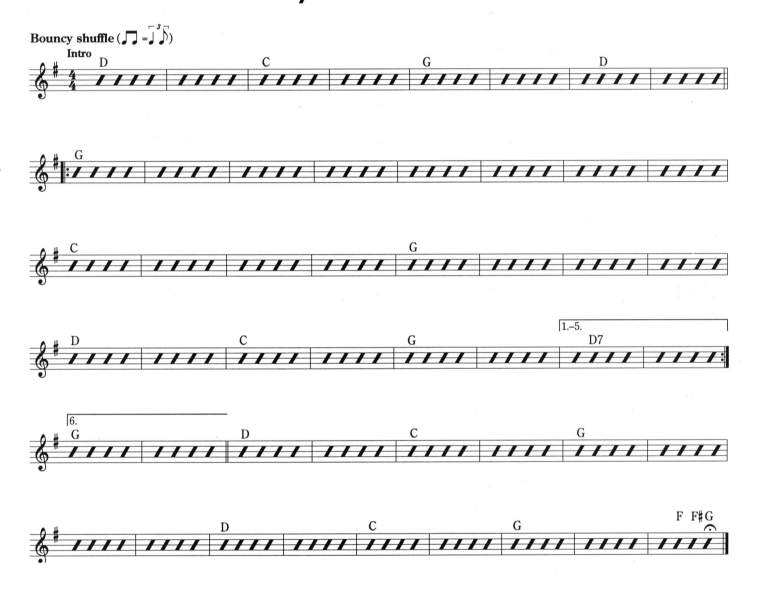

Twelve-Bar Very Slow Swing in G

C harmonica, second position

It's about time that we got around to a slow blues. Here it is!

Pattern 1: Intro riff
Lay this down over the intro.

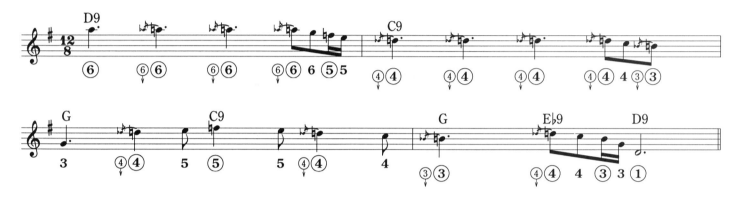

Pattern 2: Solo suggestion
For use over the first six bars of the cycle.

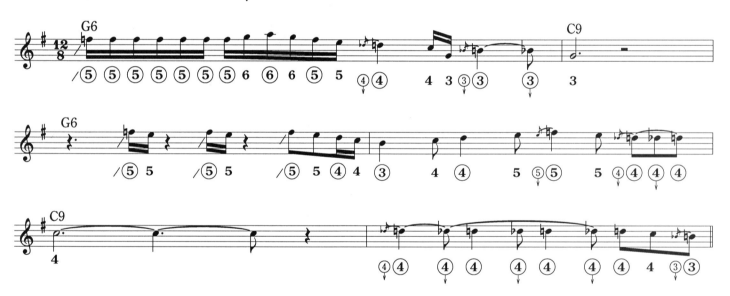

Pattern 3: Another solo suggestion
Play over the second six bars of the cycle.

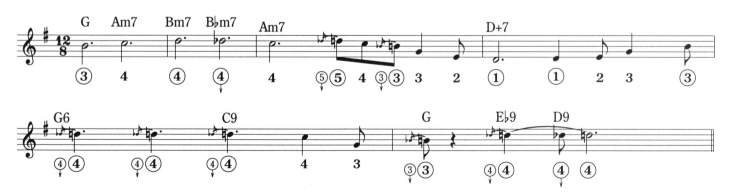

Pattern 4: Coda riff

For the last two bars of the tune.

Twelve-Bar Very Slow Swing in G

The Hindenburg Medley

A harmonica, second position

And, finally, we end with a hard rock track in the style of Led Zeppelin. Play long, wailing notes to get the proper effect.

Pattern 1: [A] section solo suggestion

Feel free to "lay out" during the intro, coming in with lines like these in the [A] section.

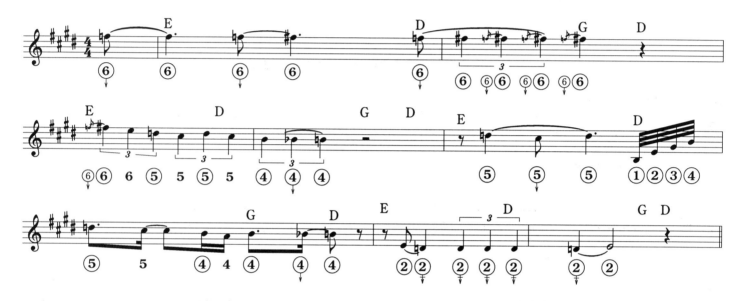

Pattern 2: [B] section solo suggestion

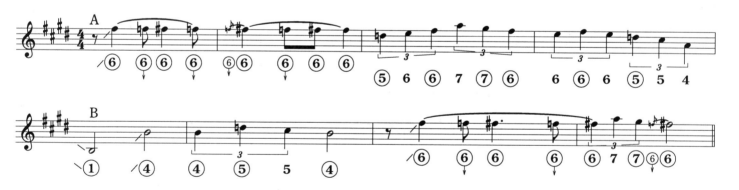

Pattern 3: Coda riff idea

Let us remind you one last time to experiment and to use the suggested patterns to create your own licks and solos.

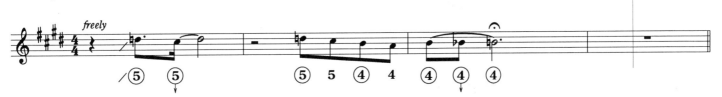

The Hindenburg Medley

Now Available!

THE Jam Trax GUITAR METHOD

Welcome to the most modern and progressive guitar method available!
All of the examples and songs included have been carefully selected in order to make
learning easy. Learn the basics of guitar playing in a way that will have you quickly jamming
with the live back-up tracks included on the CD. All examples are written in standard
notation and tablature, as well as easy-to-follow rhythmic notation.

Book 1

Basic Theory and Notation—Simple Chords and Progressions—Twelve-Bar Blues
Progression—Rhythm Studies—Basic Scale Studies—Introduction to Soloing—
and much more!

Book 2

More on Rhythm and Lead Playing—Combining Chord Shapes—More Song, Sound-Alike
Chord Progressions—Playing Tips—Live Back-Up Tracks—
and much more!

Omnibus Edition

This all-in-one volume contains the complete text, examples, and CDs of Books 1 and 2.

Also available:
JamTrax interactive book and CD packages.

Practice soloing and learn to improvise in your favorite style by jamming with the live
back-up band on the *JamTrax* CD. Learn the techniques of the professionals!
The *JamTrax* books provide suggested scales, chords, riffs, and progressions
in standard notation and tablature.

We're ready to jam when you are!

Available at your favorite music store or call 914.469.2271 for ordering information